But Mom, What is a System?

Dr. Federica Robinson-Bryant

But Mom, What is a System?

Published by Denotion Research Group
www.DenotionResearch.com

Cover & Illustrations by Tullip Studio

ISBN:
978-1-958634-39-4 (2nd edition)
978-1-958634-17-2 (1st edition)
978-1-958634-18-9 (eBook)

Printed in United States
2nd Edition

Dedication

To the believers, the lifters, and the propellers:
this book is for you. We all can use a little support
to reach our greatest potential.

The school bell rang, and I couldn't wait to tell my mom what happened in class today. My teacher asked what a system was, and I knew just what to say!

The system may just naturally exist,
but many have been engineered.
That just means they are designed and built for a
purpose, and are toward a specific task geared.

Look at the park!
The smooth path connects to the playground
where we swing and slide.
The big green trees give plenty shade
where we can play and hide.

The cool pond is where the ducks
endlessly quack and swim.
All these parts work together to form the system.

"But Mom, what is a system?" my sister raised her plea.
I continued to recall the moment in class to share my understanding.

The car, bus, van, and truck are all systems, you see.
Each vehicle has many parts working hard,
taking us wherever we need to be.

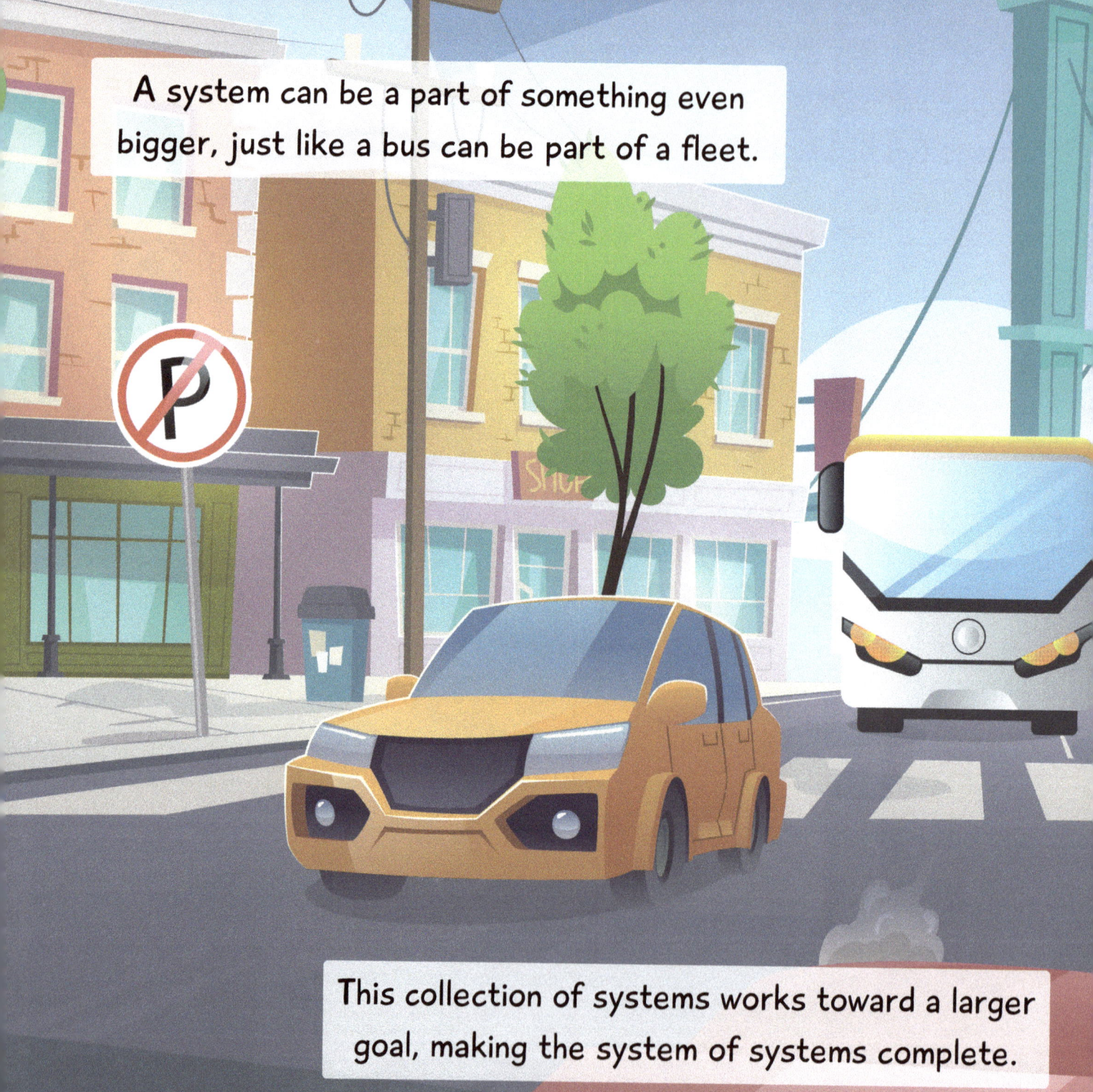

A system can be a part of something even bigger, just like a bus can be part of a fleet.

This collection of systems works toward a larger goal, making the system of systems complete.

There are many different ways to sort by type, or classify for that matter.

Some systems have many parts,
rather **COMPLEX** that's true.

While other systems are very **SIMPLE**, with only just a few.

Like gadgets in the kitchen,
some systems can be **SMALL!**

Yet others can be very **BIG**,
serving not one but all.

Some systems are **CLOSED**, like an insulated bottle, and keep everything inside.

Other systems are **OPEN**,
with things going not only in but outside.

PHYSICAL systems are things we can touch, like a Lego tower with a tilt.

Some systems are **ABSTRACT** ideas in our minds, like how some things were built.

Some systems are **MAN-MADE** in a lab, like a thermometer to check your temperature.

But other systems are **NATURAL**, like the human body, and are mysteriously made by nature.

Some systems like a gaming console, are **PERSONAL USE** so made just for you!

While **ENTERPRISE** systems send data across great distances for others to also use.

Some systems are a **PRODUCT** that can be bought, like a smart recycling bin.

But some systems are a **SERVICE** provided, like community trash collection.

Some systems are part of our planet **EARTH**, like majestic mountains and lakes.

And some systems feature stars, planets, and moons, and are way out in **SPACE**.

Vocabulary

Abstract System

Classify

Closed System

Complex System

Data

Design

Earth System

Efficiency

Engineered

Enterprise System

Man-made System

Natural System

Open System

Personal Use System

Physical System

Product System

Purpose

Regulate

Safety

Service System

Simple System

Small System

Smart

Space System

System

System of Systems